Sganarelle by Moliere

Or, The Self-Deceived Husband

Sganarelle; Ou, Le Cocu Imaginaire

A COMEDY IN ONE ACT

Jean-Baptiste Poquelin is better known to us by his stage name of Molière. He was born in Paris, to a prosperous well-to-do family on 15th January 1622.

In 1631, his father purchased from the court of Louis XIII the posts of "valet of the King's chamber and keeper of carpets and upholstery" which Molière assumed in 1641. The benefits included only three months' work per annum for which he was paid 300 livres and also provided a number of lucrative contracts.

However in June 1643, at 21, Molière abandoned this for his first love; a career on the stage. He partnered with the actress Madeleine Béjart, to found the Illustre Théâtre at a cost of 630 livres. Unfortunately despite their enthusiasm, effort and ambition the troupe went bankrupt in 1645.

Molière and Madeleine now began again and spent the next dozen years touring the provincial circuit. His journey back to the sacred land of Parisian theatres was slow but by 1658 he performed in front of the King at the Louvre.

From this point Molière both wrote and acted in a large number of productions that caused both outrage and applause. His many attacks on social conventions, the church, hypocrisy and other areas whilst also writing a large number of comedies, farces, tragicomedies, comédie-ballets are the stuff of legend.

'Tartuffe', 'The Misanthrope', 'The Miser' and 'The School for Wives' are but some of his classics.

His death was as dramatic as his life. Molière suffered from pulmonary tuberculosis. One evening he collapsed on stage in a fit of coughing and haemorrhaging while performing in the last play he'd written, in which, ironically, he was playing the hypochondriac Argan, in 'The Imaginary Invalid'.

Molière insisted on completing his performance.

Afterwards he collapsed again with another, larger haemorrhage and was taken home. Priests were sent for to administer the last rites. Two priests refused to visit. A third arrived too late. On 17th February 1673, Jean-Baptiste Poquelin, forever to be known as Molière, was pronounced dead in Paris. He was 51.

Index of Contents

DRAMATIS PERSONÆ
SCENE.—A PUBLICK PLACE IN PARIS.
SGANARELLE: OR THE SELF-DECEIVED HUSBAND, (SGANARELLE: OU LE COCU IMAGINAIRE)

INTRODUCTORY NOTES

Six months after the brilliant success of the Précieuses Ridicules, Molière brought out at the Théâtre du Petit-Bourbon a new comedy, called Sganarelle, ou le Cocu Imaginaire, which I have translated by Sganarelle, or the self-deceived Husband. It has been said that Molière owed the first idea of this piece to an Italian farce, Il Ritratto ovvero Arlichino cornuto per opinione, but, as it has never been printed, it is difficult to decide at the present time whether or not this be true. The primary idea of the play is common to many commedia dell' arte, whilst Molière has also been inspired by such old authors as Noël Du Fail, Rabelais, those of the Quinze joyes de Mariage, of the Cent nouvelles Nouvelles, and perhaps others.

The plot of Sganarelle is ingenious and plausible; every trifle becomes circumstantial evidence, and is received as conclusive proof both by the husband and wife. The dialogue is sprightly throughout, and the anxious desire of Sganarelle to kill his supposed injurer, whilst his cowardice prevents him from executing his valorous design, is extremely ludicrous. The chief aim of our author appears to have been to show how dangerous it is to judge with too much haste, especially in those circumstances where passion may either augment or diminish the view we take of certain objects. This truth, animated by a great deal of humour and wit, drew crowds of spectators for forty nights, though the play was brought out in summer and the marriage of the young king kept the court from Paris.

The style is totally different from that employed in the Précieuses Ridicules, and is a real and very good specimen of the style gaulois adapted to the age in which Molière lived. He has often been blamed for not having followed up his success of the Précieuses Ridicules by a comedy in the same style, but Molière did not want to make fresh enemies. It appears to have been a regular and set purpose with him always to produce something farcical after a creation which provoked either secret or open hostility, or even violent opposition.

Sganarelle appears in this piece for the first time, if we except the farce, or rather sketch, of the Médecin volant, where in reality nothing is developed, but everything is in mere outline. But in Sganarelle Molière has created a character that is his own just as much as Falstaff belongs to Shakespeare, Sancho Panza to Cervantes, or Panurge to Rabelais. Whether Sganarelle is a servant, a husband, the father of Lucinde, the brother of Ariste, a guardian, a faggot-maker, a doctor, he always represents the ugly side of human nature, an antiquated, grumpy, sullen, egotistical, jealous, grovelling, frightened character, ever and anon raising a laugh on account of his boasting, mean, morose, odd qualities. Molière was, at the time he wrote Sganarelle, more than thirty years old, and could therefore no longer successfully represent Mascarille as the rollicking servant of the Blunderer.

This farce was published by a certain Mr. Neufvillenaine, who was so smitten by it that, after having seen it represented several times, he knew it by heart, wrote it out, and published it, accompanied by a running commentary, which is not worth much, and preceded by a letter to a friend in which he extols its beauties. Molière got, in 1663, his name inserted, instead of that of Neufvillenaine, in the privilége du roi.

Mr. Henry Baker, the translator of this play, in the "Select Comedies of M. de Molière, London, 1732," oddly dedicates it to Miss Wolstenholme in the following words:—

MADAM,

Be so good to accept this little Present as an Instance of my high Esteem. Whoever has any Knowledge of the French Language, or any Taste for COMEDY, must needs distinguish the Excellency of Moliére's Plays: one of which is here translated. What the English may be, I leave others to determine; but the ORIGINAL, which you receive along with it, is, I am certain, worthy your Perusal.

Tho' what You read, at present, is called a DEDICATION, it is, perhaps, the most unlike one of any thing You ever saw: for, You'll find not one Word, in Praise, either of Your blooming Youth, Your agreeable Person, Your genteel Behaviour, Your easy Temper, or Your good Sense... and, the Reason is, that I cannot for my Life bring myself to such a Degree of Impertinence, as to sit down with a solemn Countenance, and Take upon me to inform the World, that the Sun is bright, and that the Spring is lovely.

My Knowledge of You from Your Infancy, and the many Civilities I am obliged for to Your Family, will, I hope, be an Excuse for this Presumption in,

MADAM, Your most obedient humble servant

Henry Baker
Enfield,
Jan. 1st 1731-2.

This play seems to have induced several English playwrights to imitate it. First, we have Sir William D'Avenant's The Playhouse to be Let, of which the date of the first performance is uncertain. According to the Biographia Britannica, it was "a very singular entertainment, composed of five acts, each being a distinct performance. The first act is introductory, shows the distress of the players in the time of vacation, that obliges them to let their house, which several offer to take for different purposes; amongst the rest a Frenchman, who had brought over a troop of his countrymen to act a farce. This is performed in the second act, which is a translation of Moliére's Sganarelle, or the Cuckold Conceit; all in broken French to make the people laugh. The third act is a sort of comic opera, under the title of The History of Sir Francis Drake. The fourth act is a serious opera, representing the cruelties of the Spaniards in Peru. The fifth act is a burlesque in Heroicks on the Amours of Cæsar and Cleopatra, has a great deal of wit and humour, and was often acted afterwards by itself."

With the exception of the first act, all the others, which are separate and distinct, but short dramatic pieces, were written in the time of Oliver Cromwell, and two of them at least were performed at the Cockpit, when Sir William D'Avenant had obtained permission to present his entertainments of music and perspective in scenes.

The second imitation of Sganarelle is "Tom Essence, or the Modish Wife, a Comedy as it is acted at the Duke's Theatre, 1677. London, printed by T. M. for W. Cademan, at the Pope's Head, in the Lower Walk of the New Exchange in the Strand, 1677." This play is written by a Mr. Thomas Rawlins, printer and engraver to the Mint, under Charles the First and Second, and is founded on two French comedies—- viz., Molière's Sganarelle, and Thomas Corneille's Don César d' Avalos. The prologue is too bad to be quoted, and I doubt if it can ever have been spoken on any stage. This play is written partly in blank verse, partly in prose; though very coarse, it is, on the whole, clever and witty. Old Moneylove, a credulous fool, who has a young wife (Act ii., Scene I), reminds one at times of the senator Antonio in Otway's Venice Preserved, and is, of course, deceived by the gallant Stanley; the sayings and doings of Mrs. Moneylove, who is "what she ought not to be," and the way she tricks her husband, are very racy, perhaps too much so for the taste of the present times. I do not think any dramatist would now bring upon the stage a young lady like Theodocia, daughter of old Moneylove, reading the list about Squire Careless. Tom Essence is a seller of perfumes, a "jealous coxcomb of his wife;" and Courtly is "a sober gentleman, servant to Theodocia;" these are imitations of Sganarelle and Lelio. Loveall, "a wilde debaucht blade," and Mrs. Luce, "a widdow disguis'd, and passes for Theodocia's maid," are taken from Corneille.

In the epilogue, the whole of which cannot be given, Mrs. Essence speaks the following lines:

"But now methinks a Cloak-Cabal I see,
Whose Prick-ears glow, whilst they their Jealousie
In Essence find; but Citty-Sirs, I fear,
Most of you have more cause to be severe.
We yield you are the truest Character."

Nearly all the scenes imitated in this play from Molière's Sganarelle contain nothing which merits to be reproduced.

The Perplexed Couple, or Mistake upon Mistake, as it is acted at the New Theatre in Lincolns-Inn-Fields, by the Company of Comedians, acting under Letters Patent granted by King Charles the Second. London, Printed for W. Meares at the Lamb, and F. Brown, at the Black Swan without Temple Bar, 1715, is the third imitation of Molière's Sganarelle. This comedy, printed for two gentlemen, with zoological signs, was written by a Mr. Charles Molloy, who for a long time was the editor of a well-known paper, Common Sense, in defence of Tory principles. This play had little success, and deserved to have had none, for it has no merit whatever. Our author states in the prologue:—

"The injur'd Muses, who with savage Rage,
Of late have often been expell'd a Tyrant Stage,
Here fly for Refuge; where, secure from Harms,
By you protected, shall display their Charms...
No Jest profane the guilty scene deforms,
That impious way of being dull he scorns;
No Party Cant shall here inflame the Mind,
And poison what for Pleasure was designed."

Mr. Molloy admits in the preface that "the Incident of the Picture in the Third act, something in the Fourth, and one Hint in the last Act, are taken from the Cocu Imaginaire; the rest I'm forced to subscribe to myself, for I can lay it to no Body else." I shall only remark on this, that nearly the whole play is a mere paraphrasing of Molière's Cocu Imaginaire, and several other of his plays. The scene between Leonora, the heroine, and Sterling, the old usurer and lover (Act I.), is imitated from Madelon's description in the art of making love in the Pretentious Young Ladies, and so are many others. The servant Crispin is a medley of Mascarille from The Blunderer, of Gros-René from The Love-Tiff, and of the servant of the same name in the Cocu Imaginaire; the interfering uncle of Lady Thinwit, is taken from George Dandin, whilst Sir Anthony Tainwit becomes Sganarelle. The only thing new I have been able to discover in The Perplexed Couple is the lover Octavio disguising himself as a pedlar to gain admittance to the object of his love; and old Sterling, the usurer, marrying the maid instead of the mistress. Molière's farce has been lengthened by those means into a five-act comedy, and though "no jest profane" may be found in it it is more full than usual of coarse and lewd sayings, which can hardly be called inuendoes. The play is a mistake altogether; perhaps that is the reason, its second name is called Mistake upon Mistake.

The Picture, or the Cuckold in Conceit, a Comedy in one act, by Js. Miller, is founded on Molière, and is the fourth imitation of Sganarelle. London, MDCCXLV. This play is, on the whole, a free translation of Molière's, interspersed with some songs set to music by Dr. Arne. Sganarelle is called Mr. Timothy Dotterel, grocer and common councilman; Gorgibus, Mr. Per-cent; Lelio, Mr. Heartly; Gros-René, John Broad, whilst Celia's maid is called Phillis. The Prologue, spoken by Mr. Havard, ends thus:

"...To-night we serve
A Cuckold, that the Laugh does well deserve;
A Cuckold in Conceit, by Fancy made
As mad, as by the common Course of Trade:
And more to please ye, and his Worth enhance,
He's carbonado'd a la mode de France;

Cook'd by Molière, great Master of his Trade,
From whose Receipt this Harrico was made.
But if that poignant Taste we fail to take,
That something, that a mere Receipt can't make;
Forgive the Failure—we're but Copies all,
And want the Spirit of th' Original."

The fifth and best imitation is Arthur Murphy's All in the Wrong, a comedy in five acts, first performed during the summer season of 1761, at the Theatre Royal, in Drury Lane. Though the chief idea and several of the scenes are taken from Sganarelle, yet the characters are well drawn, and the play, as a whole, very entertaining. The Prologue, written and spoken by Samuel Foote, is as follows:

"To-night, be it known to Box, Gall'ry, and Pit,
Will be open'd the best Summer-Warehouse for Wit;

[Footnote: Mr. Garrick, at this time, had let his playhouse for the summer months.]

The New Manufacture, Foote and Co., Undertakers;
Play, Pantomime, Opera, Farce,—by the Makers!
We scorn, like our brethren, our fortunes to owe
To Shakespeare and Southern, to Otway and Rowe.
Though our judgment may err, yet our justice is shewn,
For we promise to mangle no works but our own.
And moreover on this you may firmly rely,
If we can't make you laugh, that we won't make you cry.
For Roscius, who knew we were mirth-loving souls,
Has lock'd up his lightning, his daggers, and bowls.
Resolv'd that in buskins no hero shall stalk,
He has shut us quite out of the Tragedy walk.
No blood, no blank verse!—and in short we're undone,
Unless you're contented with Frolic and Fun.
If tired of her round in the Ranelagh-mill,
There should be but one female inclined to sit still;
If blind to the beauties, or sick of the squall,
A party should shun to catch cold at Vauxhall;
If at Sadler's sweet Wells the made wine should be thick,
The cheese-cakes turn sour, or Miss Wilkinson sick;
If the fume of the pipes should oppress you in June,
Or the tumblers be lame, or the bells out of tune;
I hope you will call at our warehouse in Drury;
We've a curious assortment of goods, I assure you;
Domestic and foreign, and all kinds of wares;
English cloths, Irish linnen, and French petenlairs!
If for want of good custom, or losses in trade,
The poetical partners should bankrupts be made;
If from dealings too large, we plunge deeply in debt,
And Whereas issue out in the Muses Gazette;
We'll on you our assigns for Certificates call;

Though insolvent, we're honest, and give up our all."

Otway in his very indecent play, The Soldier's Fortune, performed at Dorset Garden, 1681, has borrowed freely from Molière; namely: one scene from Sganarelle, four scenes from The School for Husbands, and a hint from The School for Wives.

The joke from The Pretentious Young Ladies, Scene xii., page 162, about "the half moon and the full moon" is repeated in the conversation between Fourbin and Bloody-Bones in The Soldier's Fortune.

Sir John Vanbrugh also translated Molière's Sganarelle, which was performed at the Queen's Theatre in the Haymarket, 1706, but has not been printed.

There was also a ballad opera played at Drury Lane April 11, 1733, called the Imaginary Cuckold, which is an imitation of Sganarelle.

DRAMATIS PERSONÆ
GORGIBUS, a citizen of Paris
LELIO, in love with Celia
SGANARELLE, a citizen of Paris and the self-deceived husband*
VILLEBREQUIN, father to Valère
GROS-RENÉ, servant to Lelio
A RELATIVE OF SGANARELLE'S WIFE
CELIA, daughter of Gorgibus
SGANARELLE'S WIFE
CELIA'S MAID

*Molière acted this part

SCENE.—A PUBLICK PLACE IN PARIS.

SGANARELLE: OR THE SELF-DECEIVED HUSBAND

(SGANARELLE: OU LE COCU IMAGINAIRE)

SCENE I

GORGIBUS, CELIA, CELIA'S MAID.

CELIA [Coming out in tears, her father following her]
Ah! never expect my heart to consent to that.

GORGIBUS

What do you mutter, you little impertinent girl? Do you suppose you can thwart my resolution? Have I not absolute power over you? And shall your youthful brain control my fatherly discretion by foolish arguments? Which of us two has most right to command the other? Which of us two, you or I, is, in your opinion, best able to judge what is advantageous for you? Zounds, do not provoke me too much, or you may feel, and in a very short time too, what strength this arm of mine still possesses! Your shortest way, you obstinate minx, would be to accept without any more ado the husband intended for you; but you say, "I do not know what kind of temper he has, and I ought to think about it beforehand, if you will allow me." I know that he is heir to a large fortune; ought I therefore to trouble my head about anything else? Can this man, who has twenty thousand golden charms in his pocket to be beloved by you, want any accomplishments? Come, come, let him be what he will, I promise you that with such a sum he is a very worthy gentleman!

CELIA
Alas!

GORGIBUS
Alas, indeed! What is the meaning of that? A fine alas you have uttered just now! Look ye! If once you put me in a passion you will have plenty of opportunities for shouting alas! This comes of that eagerness of yours to read novels day and night; your head is so full of all kinds of nonsense about love, that you talk of God much less than of Clélie. Throw into the fire all these mischievous books, which are every day corrupting the minds of so many young people; instead of such trumpery, read, as you ought to do, the Quatrains of Pibrac and the learned memorandum-books of Councillor Matthieu, a valuable work and full of fine sayings for you to learn by heart; the Guide for Sinners is also a good book. Such writings teach people in a short time how to spend their lives well, and if you had never read anything but such moral books you would have known better how to submit to my commands.

CELIA
Do you suppose, dear father, I can ever forget that unchangeable affection I owe to Lelio? I should be wrong to dispose of my hand against your will, but you yourself engaged me to him.

GORGIBUS
Even if you were engaged ever so much, another man has made his appearance whose fortune annuls your engagement. Lelio is a pretty fellow, but learn that there is nothing that does not give way to money, that gold will make even the most ugly charming, and that without it everything else is but wretchedness. I believe you are not very fond of Valère, but though you do not like him as a lover, you will like him as a husband. The very name of husband endears a man more than is generally supposed, and love is often a consequence of marriage. But what a fool I am to stand arguing when I possess the absolute right to command. A truce then, I tell you, to your impertinence; let me have no more of your foolish complaints. This evening Valère intends to visit you, and if you do not receive him well, and look kindly upon him, I shall... but I will say no more on this subject.

SCENE II

CELIA, CELIA'S MAID.

CELIA'S MAID

What, madam! you refuse positively what so many other people would accept with all their heart! You answer with tears a proposal for marriage, and delay for a long time to say a "yes" so agreeable to hear! Alas! why does some one not wish to marry me? I should not need much entreaty: and so far from thinking it any trouble to say "yes" once, believe me I would very quickly say it a dozen times. Your brother's tutor was quite right when, as we were talking about worldly affairs, he said, "A woman is like the ivy, which grows luxuriantly whilst it clings closely to the tree, but never thrives if it be separated from it." Nothing can be truer, my dear mistress, and I, miserable sinner, have found it out. Heaven rest the soul of my poor Martin! when he was alive my complexion was like a cherub's; I was plump and comely, my eyes sparkled brightly, and I felt happy: now I am doleful. In those pleasant times, which flew away like lightning, I went to bed, in the very depth of winter, without kindling a fire in the room; even airing the sheets appeared then to me ridiculous; but now I shiver even in the dogdays. In short, madam, believe me there is nothing like having a husband at night by one's side, were it only for the pleasure of hearing him say, "God bless you," whenever one may happen to sneeze.

CELIA
Can you advise me to act so wickedly as to forsake Lelio and take up with this ill-shaped fellow?

CELIA'S MAID
Upon my word, your Lelio is a mere fool to stay away the very time he is wanted; his long absence makes me very much suspect some change in his affection.

CELIA [Showing her the portrait of **LELIO**]
Oh! do not distress me by such dire forebodings! Observe carefully the features of his face; they swear to me an eternal affection; after all, I would not willingly believe them to tell a falsehood, but that he is such as he is here limned by art, and that his affection for me remains unchanged.

CELIA'S MAID
To be sure, these features denote a deserving lover, whom you are right to regard tenderly.

CELIA
And yet I must—Ah! support me.

[She lets fall the portrait of Lelio.

CELIA'S MAID
Madam, what is the cause of... Heavens! she swoons. Oh! make haste! help! help!

SCENE III

CELIA, SGANARELLE, CELIA'S MAID.

SGANARELLE
What is the matter? I am here.

CELIA'S MAID
My lady is dying.

SGANARELLE
What! is that all? You made such a noise, I thought the world was at an end. Let us see, however. Madam, are you dead? Um! she does not say one word.

CELIA'S MAID
I shall fetch somebody to carry her in; be kind enough to hold her so long.

SCENE IV

CELIA, SGANARELLE, SGANARELLE'S WIFE.

SGANARELLE [Passing his hand over **CELIA'S** bosom]
She is cold all over, and I do not know what to say to it. Let me draw a little nearer and try whether she breathes or not. Upon my word, I cannot tell, but I perceive still some signs of life.

SGANARELLE'S WIFE [Looking from the window]
Ah! what do I see? My husband, holding in his arms... But I shall go down; he is false to me most certainly; I should be glad to catch him.

SGANARELLE
She must be assisted very quickly; she would certainly be in the wrong to die. A journey to another world is very foolish, so long as a body is able to stay in this.

[He carries her in.

SCENE V

SGANARELLE'S WIFE, alone.
He has suddenly left this spot; his flight has disappointed my curiosity; but I doubt no longer that he is unfaithful to me; the little I have seen sufficiently proves it. I am no longer astonished that he returns my modest love with strange coldness; the ungrateful wretch reserves his caresses for others, and starves me in order to feed their pleasures. This is the common way of husbands; they become indifferent to what is lawful; at the beginning they do wonders, and seem to be very much in love with us, but the wretches soon grow weary of our fondness, and carry elsewhere what is due to us alone. Oh! how it vexes me that the law will not permit us to change our husband as we do our linen! That would be very convenient; and, troth, I know some women whom it would please as much as myself.

[Taking up the picture which **CELIA** had let fall.

But what a pretty thing has fortune sent me here; the enamel of it is most beautiful, the workmanship delightful; let me open it?

SCENE VI

SGANARELLE, SGANARELLE'S WIFE.

SGANARELLE [Thinking himself alone]
They thought her dead, but it was nothing at all! She is already recovering and nearly well again. But I see my wife.

SGANARELLE'S WIFE [Thinking herself alone]
O Heaven! It is a miniature, a fine picture of a handsome man.

SGANARELLE [Aside, and looking over his wife's shoulder]
What is this she looks at so closely? This picture bodes my honour little good. A very ugly feeling of jealousy begins to creep over me.

SGANARELLE'S WIFE [Not seeing her husband]
I never saw anything more beautiful in my life! The workmanship is even of greater value than the gold! Oh, how sweet it smells!

SGANARELLE [Aside]
The deuce! She kisses it! I am victimized!

SGANARELLE'S WIFE [Continues her Monologue]
I think it must be a charming thing to have such a fine-looking man for a sweetheart; if he should urge his suit very much the temptation would be great. Alas! why have I not a handsome man like this for my husband instead of my booby, my clod-hopper...?

SGANARELLE [Snatching the portrait from her]
What, hussey! have I caught you in the very act, slandering your honourable and darling husband? According to you, most worthy spouse, and everything well considered, the husband is not as good as the wife? In Beelzebub's name (and may he fly away with you), what better match could you wish for? Is there any fault to be found with me? It seems that this shape, this air, which everybody admires; this face, so fit to inspire love, for which a thousand fair ones sigh both night and day; in a word, my own delightful self, by no manner of means pleases you. Moreover, to satisfy your ravenous appetite you add to the husband the relish of a gallant.

SGANARELLE'S WIFE
I see plainly the drift of your jocular remarks, though you do not clearly express yourself. You expect by these means...

SGANARELLE
Try to impose upon others, not upon me, I pray you. The fact is evident; I have in my hands a convincing proof of the injury I complain of.

SGANARELLE'S WIFE
I am already too angry, and do not wish you to make me more so by any fresh insult. Hark ye, do not imagine that you shall keep this pretty thing; consider...

SGANARELLE

I am seriously considering whether I shall break your neck. I wish I had but the original of this portrait in my power as much as I have the copy.

SGANARELLE'S WIFE

Why?

SGANARELLE

For nothing at all, dear, sweet object of my love! I am very wrong to speak out; my forehead ought to thank you for many favours received.

[Looking at the portrait of **LELIO**.

There he is, your darling, the pretty bed-fellow, the wicked incentive of your secret flame, the merry blade with whom...

SGANARELLE'S WIFE

With whom? Go on.

SGANARELLE

With whom, I say... I am almost bursting with vexation.

SGANARELLE'S WIFE

What does the drunken sot mean by all this?

SGANARELLE

You know but too well, Mrs. Impudence. No one will call me any longer Sganarelle, but every one will give me the title of Signor Cornutus; my honor is gone, but to reward you, who took it from me, I shall at the very least break you an arm or a couple of ribs.

SGANARELLE'S WIFE

How dare you talk to me thus?

SGANARELLE

How dare you play me these devilish pranks?

SGANARELLE'S WIFE

What devilish pranks? Say what you mean.

SGANARELLE

Oh! It is not worth complaining of. A stag's top-knot on my head is indeed a very pretty ornament for everybody to come and look at.

SGANARELLE'S WIFE

After you have insulted your wife so grossly as to excite her thirst for vengeance, you stupidly imagine you can prevent the effects of it by pretending to be angry? Such insolence was never before known on the like occasion. The offender is the person who begins the quarrel.

SGANARELLE

Oh! what a shameless creature! To see the confident behaviour of this woman, would not any one suppose her to be very virtuous?

SGANARELLE'S WIFE

Away, go about your business, wheedle your mistresses, tell them you love them, caress them even, but give me back my picture, and do not make a jest of me.

[She snatches the picture from him and runs away.

SGANARELLE

So you think to escape me; but I shall get hold of it again in spite of you.

SCENE VII

LELIO, GROS-RENÉ.

GROS-RENÉ

Here we are at last; but, sir, if I might be so bold, I should like you to tell me one thing.

LELIO

Well, speak.

GROS-RENÉ

Are you possessed by some devil or other, that you do not sink under such fatigues as these? For eight whole days we have been riding long stages, and have not been sparing of whip and spur to urge on confounded screws, whose cursed trot shook us so very much that, for my part, I feel as if every limb was out of joint; without mentioning a worse mishap which troubles me very much in a place I will not mention. And yet, no sooner are you at your journey's end, than you go out well and hearty, without taking rest, or eating the least morsel.

LELIO

My haste may well be excused, for I am greatly alarmed about the report of Celia's marriage. You know I adore her, and, before everything, I wish to hear if there is any truth in this ominous rumour.

GROS-RENÉ

Ay, sir, but a good meal would be of great use to you to discover the truth or falsehood of this report; doubtless you would become thereby much stronger to withstand the strokes of fate. I judge by my own self, for, when I am fasting, the smallest disappointment gets hold of me and pulls me down; but when I have eaten sufficiently my soul can resist anything, and the greatest misfortunes cannot depress it. Believe me, stuff yourself well, and do not be too cautious. To fortify you under whatever misfortune may do, and in order to prevent sorrow from entering your heart, let it float in plenty of wine.

LELIO

I cannot eat.

GROS-RENÉ
[Aside]
I can eat very well indeed; If it is not true may I be struck dead! (Aloud). For all that, your dinner shall be ready presently.

LELIO
Hold your tongue, I command you.

GROS-RENÉ
How barbarous is that order!

LELIO
I am not hungry, but uneasy.

GROS-RENÉ
And I am hungry and uneasy as well, to see that a foolish love-affair engrosses all your thoughts.

LELIO
Let me but get some information about my heart's delight, and without troubling me more, go and take your meal if you like.

GROS-RENÉ
I never say nay when a master commands.

SCENE VIII

LELIO, alone.
No, no, my mind is tormented by too many terrors; the father has promised me Celia's hand, and she has given me such proofs of her love that I need not despair.

SCENE IX

SGANARELLE, LELIO.

SGANARELLE [Not seeing **LELIO**, and holding the portrait in his hand]
I have got it. I can now at my leisure look at the countenance of the rascal who causes my dishonour. I do not know him at all.

LELIO [Aside]
Heavens! what do I see? If that be my picture, what then must I believe?

SGANARELLE [Not seeing **LELIO**]
Ah! poor Sganarelle! your reputation is doomed, and to what a sad fate! Must...

[Perceiving that **LELIO** observes him he goes to the other side of the stage.

LELIO [Aside]
This pledge of my love cannot have left the fair hands to which I gave it, without startling my faith in her.

SGANARELLE [Aside]
People will make fun of me henceforth by holding up their two fingers; songs will be made about me, and every time they will fling in my teeth that scandalous affront, which a wicked wife has printed upon my forehead.

LELIO [Aside]
Do I deceive myself?

SGANARELLE [Aside]
Oh! Jade! were you impudent enough to cuckold me in the flower of my age? The wife too of a husband who may be reckoned handsome! and must be a monkey, a cursed addle-pated fellow...

LELIO [Aside, looking still at the portrait in **SGANARELE'S**]
I am not mistaken; it is my very picture.

SGANARELLE [Turning his back towards him]
This man seems very inquisitive.

LELIO [Aside]
I am very much surprised.

SGANARELLE
What would he be at?

LELIO [Aside]
I will speak to him. [Aloud] May I...

[**SGANARELLE** goes farther off.

I say, let me have one word with you.

SGANARELLE [Aside, and moving still farther]
What does he wish to tell me now?

LELIO
Will you inform me by what accident that picture came into your hands?

SGANARELLE [Aside]
Why does he wish to know? But I am thinking...

[Looking at **LELIO** and at the portrait in his hand.

Oh! upon my word, I know the cause of his anxiety; I no longer wonder at his surprise. This is my man, or rather, my wife's man.

LELIO
Pray, relieve my distracted mind, and tell me how you come by...

SGANARELLE
Thank Heaven, I know what disturbs you; this portrait, which causes you some uneasiness, is your very likeness, and was found in the hands of a certain acquaintance of yours; the soft endearments which have passed between that lady and you are no secret to me. I cannot tell whether I have the honour to be known by your gallant lordship in this piece of gallantry; but henceforth, be kind enough to break off an intrigue, which a husband may not approve of; and consider that the holy bonds of wedlock...

LELIO
What do you say? She from whom you received this pledge...

SGANARELLE
Is my wife, and I am her husband.

LELIO
Her husband?

SGANARELLE
Yes, her husband, I tell you. Though married I am far from merry; you, sir, know the reason of it; this very moment I am going to inform her relatives about this affair.

SCENE X

LELIO, alone.
Alas! what have I heard! The report then was true that her husband was the ugliest of all his sex. Even if your faithless lips had never sworn me more than a thousand times eternal love, the disgust you should have felt at such a base and shameful choice might have sufficiently secured me against the loss of your affection... But this great insult, and the fatigues of a pretty long journey, produce all at once such a violent effect upon me, that I feel faint, and can hardly bear up under it.

SCENE XI

LELIO, SGANARELLE'S WIFE.

SGANARELLE'S WIFE
In spite of me, my wretch...

[Seeing **LELIO.**

Good lack! what ails you? I perceive, sir, you are ready to faint away.

LELIO
It is an illness that has attacked me quite suddenly.

SGANARELLE'S WIFE
I am afraid you shall faint; step in here, and stay until you are better.

LELIO
For a moment or two I will accept of your kindness.

SCENE XII

SGANARELLE, A RELATIVE OF SGANARELLE'S WIFE.

RELATIVE
I commend a husband's anxiety in such a case, but you take fright a little too hastily. All that you have told me against her, kinsman, does not prove her guilty. It is a delicate subject, and no one should ever be accused of such a crime unless it can be fully proved.

SGANARELLE
That is to say, unless you see it.

RELATIVE
Too much haste leads us to commit mistakes. Who can tell how this picture came into her hands, and, after all, whether she knows the man? Seek a little more information, and if it proves to be as you suspect, I shall be one of the first to punish her offence.

SCENE XIII

SGANARELLE, alone.
Nothing could be said fairer; it is really the best way to proceed cautiously. Perhaps I have dreamt of horns without any cause, and the perspiration has covered my brow rather prematurely. My dishonour is not at all proved by that portrait which frightened me so much. Let me endeavour then by care...

SCENE XIV

SGANARELLE, SGANARELLE'S WIFE, standing at the door of her house, with **LELIO**.

SGANARELLE [Aside seeing them]
Ha! what do I see? Zounds! there can be no more question about the portrait, for upon my word here stands the very man, in propria persona.

SGANARELLE'S WIFE

You hurry away too fast, sir; if you leave us so quickly, you may perhaps have a return of your illness.

LELIO

No, no, I thank you heartily for the kind assistance you have rendered me.

SGANARELLE [Aside]

The deceitful woman is to the last polite to him.

[**SGANARELLE'S WIFE** goes into the house again.

SCENE XV

SGANARELLE, LELIO.

SGANARELLE

He has seen me, let us hear what he can say to me.

LELIO [Aside]

Oh! my soul is moved! this sight inspires me with... but I ought to blame this unjust resentment, and only ascribe my sufferings to my merciless fate; yet I cannot help envying the success that has crowned his passion.

[Approaching **SGANARELLE**.

O too happy mortal in having so beautiful a wife.

SCENE XVI

SGANARELLE, CELIA, at her window, seeing **LELIO** go away.

SGANARELLE [Alone]

This confession is pretty plain. His extraordinary speech surprises me as much as if horns had grown upon my head.

[Looking at the side where **LELIO** went off.

Go your way, you have not acted at all like an honourable man.

CELIA [Aside, entering]

Who can that be? Just now I saw Lelio. Why does he conceal his return from me?

SGANARELLE [Without seeing **CELIA**]

"O too happy mortal in having so beautiful a wife!" Say rather, unhappy mortal in having such a disgraceful spouse through whose guilty passion, it is now but too clear, I have been cuckolded without any feeling of compassion. Yet I allow him to go away after such a discovery, and stand with my arms folded like a regular silly-billy! I ought at least to have knocked his hat off, thrown stones at him, or mud on his cloak; to satisfy my wrath I should rouse the whole neighbourhood, and cry, "Stop, thief of my honour!"

CELIA [To **SGANARELLE**]
Pray, sir, how came you to know this gentleman who went away just now and spoke to you?

SGANARELLE
Alas! madam, it is not I who am acquainted with him; it is my wife.

CELIA
What emotion thus disturbs your mind?

SGANARELLE
Do not blame me; I have sufficient cause for my sorrow; permit me to breathe plenty of sighs.

CELIA
What can be the reason of this uncommon grief?

SGANARELLE
If I am sad it is not for a trifle: I challenge other people not to grieve, if they found themselves in my condition. You see in me the model of unhappy husbands. Poor Sganarelle's honour is taken from him; but the loss of my honour would be small—they deprive me of my reputation also.

CELIA
How do they do that?

SGANARELLE
That fop has taken the liberty to cuckold me—saving your presence, madam—and this very day my own eyes have been witness to a private interview between him and my wife.

CELIA
What? He who just now...

SGANARELLE
Ay, ay, it is he who brings disgrace upon me; he is in love with my wife, and my wife is in love with him.

CELIA
Ah! I find I was right when I thought his returning secretly only concealed some base design; I trembled the minute I saw him, from a sad foreboding of what would happen.

SGANARELLE
You espouse my cause with too much kindness, but everybody is not so charitably disposed; for many, who have already heard of my sufferings, so far from taking my part, only laugh at me.

CELIA

Can anything be more base than this vile deed? or can a punishment be discovered such as he deserves? Does he think he is worthy to live, after polluting himself with such treachery? O Heaven! is it possible?

SGANARELLE

It is but too true.

CELIA

O traitor, villain, deceitful, faithless wretch!

SGANARELLE

What a kind-hearted creature!

CELIA

No, no, hell has not tortures enough to punish you sufficiently for your guilt!

SGANARELLE

How well she talks!

CELIA

Thus to abuse both innocence and goodness!

SGANARELLE [Sighing aloud]

Ah!

CELIA

A heart which never did the slightest action deserving of being treated with such insult and contempt.

SGANARELLE

That's true.

CELIA

Who far from... but it is too much; nor can this heart endure the thought of it without feeling on the rack.

SGANARELLE

My dear lady, do not distress yourself so much; it pierces my very soul to see you grieve so at my misfortune.

CELIA

But do not deceive yourself so far as to fancy that I shall sit down and do nothing but lament; no, my heart knows how to act in order to be avenged; nothing can divert me from it; I go to prepare everything.

SCENE XVII

SGANARELLE, alone.

May Heaven keep her for ever out of harm's way! How kind of her to wish to avenge me! Her anger at my dishonour plainly teaches me how to act. Nobody should bear such affronts as these tamely, unless indeed he be a fool. Let us therefore hasten to hunt out this rascal who has insulted me, and let me prove my courage by avenging my dishonour.

I will teach you, you rogue, to laugh at my expense, and to cuckold people without showing them any respect.

[After going three or four steps he comes back again.

But gently, if you please, this man looks as if he were very hot-headed and passionate; he may, perhaps, heaping one insult upon another, ornament my back as well as he has done my brow.

I detest, from the bottom of my heart, these fiery tempers, and vastly prefer peaceable people. I do not care to beat for fear of being beaten; a gentle disposition was always my predominant virtue: But my honour tells me that it is absolutely necessary I should avenge such an outrage as this. Let honour say whatever it likes, the deuce take him who listens. Suppose now I should play the hero, and receive for my pains an ugly thrust with a piece of cold steel quite through my stomach; when the news of my death spreads through the whole town, tell me then, my honour, shall you be the better of it.

The grave is too melancholy an abode, and too unwholesome for people who are afraid of the colic; as for me, I find, all things considered, that it is, after all, better to be a cuckold than to be dead. What harm is there in it? Does it make a man's legs crooked? does it spoil his shape? The plague take him who first invented being grieved about such a delusion, linking the honour of the wisest man to anything a fickle woman may do. Since every person is rightly held responsible for his own crimes, how can our honour, in this case, be considered criminal? We are blamed for the actions of other people. If our wives have an intrigue with any man, without our knowledge, all the mischief must fall upon our backs; they commit the crime and we are reckoned guilty. It is a villainous abuse, and indeed Government should remedy such injustice. Have we not enough of other accidents that happen to us whether we like them or not? Do not quarrels, lawsuits, hunger, thirst, and sickness sufficiently disturb the even tenour of our lives? and yet we must stupidly get it into our heads to grieve about something which has no foundation. Let us laugh at it, despise such idle fears, and be above sighs and tears. If my wife has done amiss, let her cry as much as she likes, but why should I weep when I have done no wrong? After all, I am not the only one of my fraternity, and that should console me a little. Many people of rank see their wives cajoled, and do not say a word about it. Why should I then try to pick a quarrel for an affront, which is but a mere trifle? They will call me a fool for not avenging myself, but I should be a much greater fool to rush on my own destruction.

[Putting his hand upon his stomach.

I feel, however, my bile is stirred up here; it almost persuades me to do some manly action. Ay, anger gets the better of me; it is rather too much of a good thing to be a coward too! I am resolved to be revenged upon the thief of my honour. Full of the passion which excites my ardour, and in order to make a beginning, I shall go and tell everywhere that he lies with my wife.

GORGIBUS, CELIA, CELIA'S MAID.

CELIA

Yes, I will yield willingly to so just a law, father; you can freely dispose of my heart and my hand; I will sign the marriage contract whenever you please, for I am now determined to perform my duty. I can command my own inclinations, and shall do whatever you order me.

GORGIBUS

How she pleases me by talking in this manner! Upon my word! I am so delighted that I would immediately cut a caper or two, were people not looking on, who would laugh at it. Come hither, I say, and let me embrace you; there is no harm in that; a father may kiss his daughter whenever he likes, without giving any occasion for scandal. Well, the satisfaction of seeing you so obedient has made me twenty years younger.

CELIA, CELIA'S MAID.

CELIA'S MAID

This change surprises me.

CELIA

When you come to know why I act thus, you will esteem me for it.

CELIA'S MAID

Perhaps so.

CELIA

Know then that Lelio has wounded my heart by his treacherous behaviour, and has been in this neighbourhood without...

CELIA'S MAID

Here he comes.

LELIO, CELIA, CELIA'S MAID.

LELIO

Before I take my leave of you for ever, I will at least here tell you that...

CELIA

What! are you insolent enough to speak to me again?

LELIO
I own my insolence is great, and yet your choice is such I should not be greatly to blame if I upbraided you. Live, live contented, and laugh when you think of me, as well as your worthy husband, of whom you have reason to be proud.

CELIA
Yes, traitor, I will live so, and I trust most earnestly that the thought of my happiness may disturb you.

LELIO
Why this outbreak of passion?

CELIA
You pretend to be surprised, and ask what crimes you have committed?

SCENE XXI

CELIA, LELIO, SGANARELLE, armed cap-a-pié, **CELIA'S MAID**.

SGANARELLE
I wage war, a war of extermination against this robber of my honour, who without mercy has sullied my fair name.

CELIA [To **LELIO**, pointing to **SGANARELLE**]
Look on this man, and then you will require no further answer.

LELIO
Ah! I see.

CELIA
A mere glance at him is sufficient to abash you.

LELIO
It ought rather to make you blush.

SGANARELLE
My wrath is now disposed to vent itself upon some one; my courage is at its height; if I meet him, there will be blood shed. Yes, I have sworn to kill him, nothing can keep me from doing so. Wherever I see him I will dispatch him.

[Drawing his sword halfway and approaching **LELIO**.

Right through the middle of his heart I shall thrust...

LELIO [Turning round]

Against whom do you bear such a grudge?

SGANARELLE
Against no one.

LELIO
Why are you thus in armour?

SGANARELLE
It is a dress I put on to keep the rain off. [Aside] Ah! what a satisfaction it would be for me to kill him! Let us pluck up courage to do it.

LELIO [Turning round again]
Hey?

SGANARELLE
I did not speak.
[Aside, boxing his own ears, and thumping himself to raise his courage]
Ah! I am enraged at my own cowardice! Chicken-hearted poltroon!

CELIA
What you have seen ought to satisfy you, but it appears to offend you.

LELIO
Yes through him I know you are guilty of the greatest faithlessness that ever wronged a faithful lover's heart, and for which no excuse can be found.

SGANARELLE [Aside]
Why have I not a little more courage?

CELIA
Ah, traitor, speak not to me in so unmanly and insolent a manner.

SGANARELLE [Aside]
You see, Sganarelle, she takes up your quarrel: courage, my lad, be a trifle vigorous. Now, be bold, try to make one noble effort and kill him whilst his back is turned.

LELIO [Who has moved accidentally a few steps back, meets **SGANARELLE**, who was drawing near to kill him. The latter is frightened, and retreats]
Since my words kindle your wrath, madam, I ought to show my satisfaction with what your heart approves, and here commend the lovely choice you have made.

CELIA
Yes, yes, my choice is such as cannot be blamed.

LELIO
You do well to defend it.

SGANARELLE

No doubt, she does well to defend my rights, but what you have done, sir, is not according to the laws; I have reason to complain; were I less discreet, much blood would be shed.

LELIO

Of what do you complain? And why this...

SGANARELLE

Do not say a word more. You know too well where the shoe pinches me. But conscience and a care for your own soul should remind you that my wife is my wife, and that to make her yours under my very nose is not acting like a good Christian.

LELIO

Such a suspicion is mean and ridiculous! Harbour no scruples on that point: I know she belongs to you; I am very far from being in love with...

CELIA

Oh! traitor! how well you dissemble!

LELIO

What! do you imagine I foster a thought which need disturb his mind? Would you slander me by accusing me of such a cowardly action?

CELIA

Speak, speak to himself; he can enlighten you.

SGANARELLE [To **CELIA**]

No, no, you can argue much better than I can, and have treated the matter in the right way.

SCENE XXII

CELIA, LELIO, SGANARELLE, SGANARELLE'S WIFE, CELIA'S MAID.

SGANARELLE'S WIFE [To **CELIA**]

I am not inclined, Madam, to show that I am over-jealous; but I am no fool, and can see what is going on. There are certain amours which appear very strange; you should be better employed than in seducing a heart which ought to be mine alone.

CELIA

This declaration of her love is plain enough.

SGANARELLE [To his **WIFE**]

Who sent for you, baggage? You come and scold her because she takes my part, whilst you are afraid of losing your gallant.

CELIA

Do not suppose anybody has a mind to him.

[Turning towards **LELIO**.

You see whether I have told a falsehood, and I am very glad of it.

LELIO
What can be the meaning of this?

CELIA'S MAID
Upon my word, I do not know when this entanglement will be unravelled. I have tried for a pretty long time to comprehend it, but the more I hear the less I understand. Really I think I must interfere at last.

[Placing herself between **LELIO** and **CELIA**.

Answer me one after another, and
[To **LELIO**]
—allow me to ask what do you accuse this lady of?

LELIO
That she broke her word and forsook me for another. As soon as I heard she was going to be married I hastened hither, carried away by an irrepressible love, and not believing I could be forgotten; but discovered, when I arrived here, that she was married.

CELIA'S MAID
Married! To whom?

LELIO [Pointing to **SGANARELLE**]
To him.

CELIA'S MAID
How! to him?

LELIO
Yes, to him.

CELIA'S MAID
Who told you so?

LELIO
Himself, this very day.

CELIA'S MAID [To **SGANARELLE**]
Is this true?

SGANARELLE
I? I told him I was married to my own wife.

LELIO
Just now, whilst you looked at my picture, you seemed greatly moved.

SGANARELLE
True, here it is.

LELIO [To **SGANARELLE**]
You also told me that she, from whose hands you had received this pledge of her love, was joined to you in the bonds of wedlock.

SGANARELLE
No doubt—
[Pointing to his **WIFE**]
—for I snatched it from her, and should not have discovered her wickedness had I not done so.

SGANARELLE'S WIFE
What do you mean by your groundless complaint? I found this portrait at my feet by accident. After you had stormed without telling me the cause of your rage, I saw this gentleman—
[Pointing to **LELIO**]
—nearly fainting, asked him to come in, but did not even then discover that he was the original of the picture.

CELIA
I was the cause of the portrait being lost; I let it fall when swooning, and when you—
[To **SGANARELLE**]
—kindly carried me into the house.

CELIA'S MAID
You see that without my help you had still been at a loss, and that you had some need of hellebore.

SGANARELLE [Aside]
Shall we believe all this? I have been very much frightened for my brow.

SGANARELLE'S WIFE
I have not quite recovered from my fear; however agreeable credulity may be, I am both to be deceived.

SGANARELLE [To his **WIFE**]
Well, let us mutually suppose ourselves to be people of honour. I risk more on my side than you do on yours; accept, therefore, without much ado, what I propose.

SGANARELLE'S WIFE
Be it so, but wo be to you if I discover anything.

CELIA [To **LELIO**, after whispering together]
Ye heavens! if it be so, what have I done? I ought to fear the consequences of my own anger! Thinking you false, and wishing to be avenged, I in an unhappy moment complied with my father's wishes, and but a minute since engaged myself to marry a man whose hand, until then, I always had refused. I have made a promise to my father, and what grieves me most is... But I see him coming.

LELIO

He shall keep his word with me.

SCENE XXIII

GORGIBUS, CELIA, LELIO, SGANARELLE, SGANARELLE'S WIFE, CELIA'S MAID.

LELIO

Sir, you see I have returned to this town, inflamed with the same ardour, and now I suppose you will keep your promise, which made me hope to marry Celia, and thus reward my intense love.

GORGIBUS

Sir, whom I see returned to this town inflamed with the same ardour, and who now supposes I will keep my promise, which made you hope to marry Celia, and thus reward your intense love, I am your lordship's very humble servant.

LELIO

What, sir, is it thus you frustrate my expectations?

GORGIBUS

Ay, sir, it is thus I do my duty, and my daughter obeys me too.

CELIA

My duty compels me, father, to make good your promise to him.

GORGIBUS

Is this obeying my commands as a daughter ought to do? Just now you were very kindly disposed towards Valère, but you change quickly... I see his father approaching, who certainly comes to arrange about the marriage.

SCENE XXIV

VILLEBREQUIN, GORGIBUS, CELIA, LELIO, SGANARELLE, SGANARELLE'S WIFE, CELIA'S MAID.

GORGIBUS

What brings you hither, M. Villebrequin?

VILLEBREQUIN

An important secret, which I only discovered this morning, and which completely prevents me from keeping the engagement I made with you. My son, whom your daughter was going to espouse, has deceived everybody, and been secretly married these four months past to Lise. Her friends, her fortune, and her family connections, make it impossible for me to break off this alliance; and hence I come to you....

GORGIBUS

Pray, say no more. If Valère has married some one else without your permission, I cannot disguise from you, that I myself long ago, promised my daughter Celia to Lelio, endowed with every virtue, and that his return today prevents me from choosing any other husband for her.

VILLEBREQUIN

Such a choice pleases me very much.

LELIO

This honest intention will crown my days with eternal bliss.

GORGIBUS

Let us go and fix the day for the wedding.

SGANARELLE [Alone]

Was there ever a man who had more cause to think himself victimized? You perceive that in such matters the strongest probability may create in the mind a wrong belief. Therefore remember, never to believe anything even if you should see everything.

Molière – A Short Biography

Jean-Baptiste Poquelin is better known to us by his stage name of Molière. He was born in Paris, to a prosperous well-to-do family, the son of Jean Poquelin and Marie Cressé, on 15th January 1622.

It is said that a maid, seeing him for the first time shrieked, "Le nez!", a reference to the infant's large nose. The name stuck as a family nickname from that time. At ten his mother died and his relationship with his father seems to have been lukewarm at best.

It is probable that his education started with studies in a Parisian elementary school. This was followed with his enrolment in the prestigious Jesuit Collège de Clermont, where he completed his studies in a strict academic environment but also first sampled life on the stage.

In 1631, his father purchased from the court of Louis XIII the posts of "valet de chambre ordinaire et tapissier du Roi" ("valet of the King's chamber and keeper of carpets and upholstery").

Molière assumed his father's posts in 1641. The benefits included only three months' work per annum for which he was paid 300 livres and also provided a number of lucrative contracts.

To increase the spectrum of his skills Molière also studied as a provincial lawyer around 1642, probably in Orléans, but it is not recorded if he ever qualified. Up to this date he had followed his father's plans for a career and they had served him well; he seemed destined for a career in office.

However, in June 1643, when he was 21, Molière abandoned this path for his first love; a career on the stage. He partnered with the actress Madeleine Béjart, to found the Illustre Théâtre at a cost of 630 livres.

Unfortunately, despite their enthusiasm, effort and ambition the troupe went bankrupt in 1645. Molière, now in charge, due to both his acting prowess and his legal training, had run up debts, mainly for the rent of the theatre, of 2000 livres. Molière was thrown into prison. Historians differ as to who paid the debts but after a 24-hour stint in jail Molière returned to the acting circuit.

It was at this time that he began to use the pseudonym Molière. It may also have been to spare his father the shame of having an actor in the family; a lowly profession for his status in society.

Molière and Madeleine now began with a new group of actors and spent the next dozen years touring the provincial circuit. The company slowly gained in success. Molière was also writing much of what they acted. Sadly only a few plays survive from this period among them 'The Bungler' and 'The Doctor in Love'. They represent though a distinct move away from the Italian improvisational Commedia dell'arte and highlight his use of mockery.

Armand, Prince of Conti, the governor of Languedoc, now also became his patron in return the company was named after him. Sadly for Molière the friendship later ended when Conti, having contracted syphilis from a courtesan, turned towards religion and joined Molière's enemies in the Parti des Dévots and the Compagnie de Saint Sacrement.

Molière's' journey back to the sacred land of Parisian theatres was slow. However by 1658 he performed in front of the King at the Louvre (then a theatre for hire) in Corneille's tragedy 'Nicomède' and in the farce 'Le Docteur Amoureux' (The Doctor in Love) with some success. He was awarded the title of Troupe de Monsieur (Monsieur being the honorific for the king's brother Philippe I, Duke of Orléans). With the help of Monsieur, his company was allowed to share the theatre in the large hall of the Petit-Bourbon with the famous Italian Commedia dell'arte company of Tiberio Fiorillo. The companies performed in the theatre on alternate nights.

The premiere of Molière's 'Les Précieuses Ridicules' (The Affected Young Ladies) took place at the Petit-Bourbon on 18th November 1659. It was the first of Molière's many attempts to satirize certain societal mannerisms and affectations then common in France. It won Molière the attention and the criticism of many, but alas not a large audience. He then asked Fiorillo to teach him the techniques of Commedia dell'arte. His 1660 play 'Sganarelle, ou Le Cocu imaginaire' (The Imaginary Cuckold) seems to be a tribute both to Commedia dell'arte and to his teacher.

Despite his own preference for tragedy, Molière became famous for these farces, which were generally in one act and performed after the tragedy. Some of these farces were only partly written and performed in the style of Commedia dell'arte with improvisation over a sketched out plot. He also wrote two comedies in verse, but these were less successful.

In 1660 the Petit-Bourbon was demolished to make way for the expansion of the Louvre. Molière's company decamped to the abandoned theatre in the Palais-Royal which was in the process of being refurbished. The company opened there on 20th January 1661. In order to please his patron, Monsieur, who was so enthralled with the arts that he was soon excluded from state affairs, Molière wrote and played 'Dom Garcie de Navarre ou Le Prince jaloux' (The Jealous Prince, 4th February 1661), a heroic comedy derived from a work of Cicognini's. Two other comedies of the same year were the successful 'L'École des maris' (The School for Husbands) and 'Les Fâcheux', (The Mad also known as The Bores) subtitled Comédie faite pour les divertissements du Roi (a comedy for the King's amusements) as it was performed during a series of parties that Nicolas Fouquet gave in honor of the king. These entertainments led to the arrest of Fouquet for wasting public money. He was sentenced to life imprisonment.

In parallel with 'Les Fâcheux', Molière introduced the comédies-ballets. These ballets were a transitional form of dance performance between the court ballets of Louis XIV and the art of professional theatre which was developing rapidly with the use of the proscenium stage. The comédies-ballets developed by chance when Molière was enlisted to mount both a play and a ballet in the honor of Louis XIV and found that he did not have a large enough cast to meet the needs of both. Cleverly Molière decided to combine the ballet and the play to achieve his goals. The gamble paid off handsomely. Molière was asked to produce twelve more comédies-ballets before his death. During these Molière collaborated with Pierre Beauchamp. Beauchamp codified the five balletic positions of the feet and arms and was partly responsible for the creation of the Beauchamp-Feuillet dance notation. He also collaborated with Jean-Baptiste Lully, a dancer, choreographer, and composer, whose reign at the Paris Opéra ran for fifteen years. Under Molière's command, ballet and opera became professional arts unto themselves. The comédies-ballets closely integrated dance with music and the action of the play and the style of continuity distinctly separated these performances from the court ballets of the time; additionally, the comédies-ballets demanded that both the dancers and the actors play an important role in advancing the story. Intriguingly Louis XIV played the part of an Egyptian in 'Le Mariage forcé' (1664) and also appeared as Neptune and Apollo in his retirement performance of 'Les Amants magnifiques' (1670).

On 20th February 1662 Molière married Armande Béjart, whom he believed to be the sister of Madeleine. The same year he premiered 'L'École des Femmes' (The School for Wives), widely regarded as a masterpiece. It poked fun at the limited education given to daughters of rich families and reflected on Molière's own marriage. It attracted a lot of outraged criticism and ignited the protest called the "Quarrel of L'École des femmes". Molière responded with two works: 'La Critique de "L'École des femmes"', in which he imagined the audience of the previous work attending it. It mocks them by presenting them at dinner after watching the play; it addresses all the criticism raised about the piece by presenting the critics' arguments and then dismissing them. This was the so-called Guerre comique (War of Comedy), in which the opposite side was taken by writers like Donneau de Visé, Edmé Boursault, and Montfleury.

But more serious opposition was brewing, focusing on Molière's politics and his personal life. Some in French high society protested against Molière's excessive realism and irreverence, which were causing some embarrassment. Despite this the King expressed support for him. Molière was granted a pension and the King agreed to be the godfather of Molière's first son.

Molière's friendship with Jean-Baptiste Lully influenced him towards writing his 'Le Mariage forcé' and 'La Princesse d'Élide', written for royal divertissements at the Palace of Versailles.

'Tartuffe, ou L'Imposteur' was also performed at Versailles, in 1664, and created the greatest scandal of Molière's artistic career. Its depiction of the hypocrisy of the dominant classes was taken as an outrage and violently contested. It also aroused the wrath of the Jansenists (a Catholic theological movement, that emphasized original sin, human depravity, the necessity of divine grace, and predestination). The play was banned.

Molière was always careful not to attack the monarchy in any way. He had won a position as one of the king's favourites and enjoyed his protection from the attacks of the court. When the King suggested that

Molière suspend performances of 'Tartuffe', Molière complied and quickly wrote 'Dom Juan ou le Festin de Pierre' (Don Juan, or, The Stone Banquet) to replace it. The story is of an atheist who becomes a religious hypocrite and is punished by God. But this too fell foul and was quickly suspended. The King, still keen to protect Molière became the new official sponsor of Molière's troupe.

With music by Lully, Molière presented 'Love Doctor or Medical Love'. The work was given "par ordre du Roi" (by order of the King) and was received much more warmly than its predecessors.

In 1666, 'Le Misanthrope' was produced. Molière's masterpiece. Although brimming with moral content it was little appreciated at the time and a commercial flop, forcing Molière to immediately write 'The Doctor Despite Himself', a satire against the official sciences. This was a success despite a moral treatise by the Prince of Conti, criticizing the theater in general and Molière in particular.

After the Mélicerte and the Pastorale comique, he tried again to perform a revised 'Tartuffe' in 1667, this time with the name of Panulphe or L'Imposteur. As soon as the King left Paris for a tour, the play was banned. The King finally imposed respect for 'Tartuffe' some years later, when he gained more power over the clergy.

Molière, now ill, wrote at a slower pace. 'Le Sicilien ou L'Amour peintre' (The Sicilian, or Love the Painter) was written for festivities at the castle of Saint-Germain-en-Laye, and was followed in 1668 by 'Amphitryon'.

'George Dandin, ou Le mari confondu' (The Confounded Husband) was little appreciated, but success returned with 'L'Avare' (The Miser), now very well known.

With Lully he again used music for 'Monsieur de Pourceaugnac', for 'Les Amants magnifiques' (The Magnificent Lovers), and finally for 'Le Bourgeois gentilhomme' (The Middle-Class Gentleman), another of his masterpieces. The collaboration with Lully ended with a tragédie et ballet, 'Psyché', written in collaboration with Pierre Corneille and Philippe Quinault.

In 1672, Madeleine Béjart died. It was a heavy blow to Molière who was already in declining health himself. However, he continued to write and his plays were eagerly awaited and performed. 'Les Fourberies de Scapin' (The Impostures of Scapin), a farce and a comedy in five acts was successful. The following play, 'La Comtesse d'Escarbagnas' (The Countess of Escarbagnas), is thought of as a lesser works.

'Les Femmes savantes' (The Learned Ladies) of 1672 is accepted as another masterpieces. It was born from the termination of the legal use of music in theater, (Lully had patented the opera in France and taken the best singers for his own works), so Molière returned to his traditional genre. It was a great success.

Molière suffered from pulmonary tuberculosis. One of the most famous moments in Molière's life was his last: he collapsed on stage in a fit of coughing and haemorrhaging while performing in the last play he'd written, in which, ironically, he was playing the hypochondriac Argan, in 'The Imaginary Invalid'.

Molière insisted on completing his performance.

Afterwards he collapsed again with another, larger haemorrhage and was taken home. Priests were sent for to administer the last rites. Two priests refused to visit. A third arrived too late. On 17th February 1673, Jean-Baptiste Poquelin, forever to be known as Molière, was pronounced dead in Paris. He was 51.

Under French law at the time, actors were forbidden to be buried in sacred ground. Molière's widow asked the King if Molière could be granted a normal funeral at night. The King agreed.

In his life Molière divided opinion. He was adored by the court and Parisians but loathed and reviled by moralists and the Catholic Church.

In 1792 his remains were brought to the museum of French monuments. In 1817 they were transferred to Père Lachaise Cemetery in Paris, close to those of La Fontaine.

In his 14 years in Paris, Molière singlehandedly wrote 31 of the 85 plays performed on his stage. His immensely popular legacy includes comedies, farces, tragicomedies and comédie-ballets.

Molière – A Concise Bibliography

Le Médecin Volant (1645)—The Flying Doctor
La Jalousie du Barbouillé (1650)—The Jealousy of le Barbouillé
L'Étourdi, ou le Contre-Temps(1653)—The Scatterbrain or The Bungler
L'Étourdi ou les Contretemps (1655)—The Blunderer, or, the Counterplots
Le Dépit Amoureux (16 December 1656)—The Love-Tiff
Le Docteur Amoureux (1658), 1st play performed by Molière's troupe (now lost)—The Doctor in Love
Les Précieuses Ridicules (1659)—The Affected Young Ladies
Sganarelle ou Le Cocu Imaginaire (1660)— Sganarelle or, The Self-Deceived Husband aka The Imaginary Cuckold
Dom Garcie de Navarre ou Le Prince Jaloux (1661)—Don Garcia of Navarre or the Jealous Prince
L'École des Maris (1661)—The School for Husbands
Les Fâcheux (17 August 1661)—The Mad aka The Bores
L'École des Femmes (1662; adapted into The Amorous Flea, 1964)—The School for Wives
La Jalousie du Gros-René (1663)—The Jealousy of Gros-René
La Critique de l'école des Femmes (1663)—Critique of the School for Wives
L'Impromptu de Versailles (1663)—The Versailles Impromptu
Le Mariage Forcé (1664)—The Forced Marriage
Gros-René, Petit Enfant (1664; now lost)—Gros-René, Small Child
La Princesse d'Élide (1664)—The Princess of Elid
Tartuffe ou L'Imposteur (1664)—Tartuffe, or, the Impostor
Dom Juan ou Le Festin de Pierre (1665)—Don Juan, or, The Stone Banquet (aka The Stone Guest, The Feast with the Statue)
L'Amour médecin (1665)—Love Is the Doctor aka Medical Love
Le Misanthrope ou L'Atrabilaire Amoureux (1666)—The Misanthrope, or, the Cantankerous Lover
Le Médecin Malgré Lui (1666)—The Physican in Spite of Himself aka A Doctor Despite Himself
Mélicerte (1666)
Pastorale Comique (1667)—Comic Pastoral

Le Sicilien ou L'Amour Peintre (1667)—The Sicilian, or Love the Painter
Amphitryon (1668)
George Dandin ou Le Mari Confondu (1668)—George Dandin, or, the Abashed Husband
L'Avare ou L'École du Mensonge (1668)—The Miser, or, the School for Lies
Monsieur de Pourceaugnac (1669)
Les Amants Magnifiques (1670)—The Magnificent Lovers
Le Bourgeois Gentilhomme (1670)—The Middle-Class Gentleman aka The Shopkeeper Turned Gentleman
Psyché (1671)—Psyche
Les Fourberies de Scapin (1671)—The Impostures of Scapin
La Comtesse d'Escarbagnas (1671)—The Countess of Escarbagnas
Les Femmes Savantes (1672)—The Learned Ladies aka The Learned Women
Le Malade Imaginaire (1673)—The Imaginary Invalid